SIX STRATEGIES FOR TAKING BACK MEMPHIS

A Unique Icon

Diane Winbush

Six Strategies for Taking Back Memphis

A Unique Icon

City of Memphis

ISBN-13: 978-1535435468

ISBN-10: 1535435461

References: Memphis Travel

Scripture References: King James Version Bible Copyright © 2016

City of Memphis

Acknowledgements

We acknowledge the Mayor of Memphis 2016; Mayor Jim Strickland for taking a stand to win back this great icon. It takes a leadership of a winning mindset to develop a plan for this great city. We appreciate his run for office of mayor to be that man to just that.

City of Memphis

Table of Contents

Origin of Memphis

City of Memphis

Memphis' first settlers were Native Americans who were drawn to the area's bluffs overlooking the river. By building their settlements on the Fourth Chickasaw Bluff, it protected them from flooding, and the mighty river allowed them easy transportation access.

When the explorer Hernando Desoto and his army arrived here in 1541, they were the first Europeans to see the lower half of the river. They set up camp near the site of Memphis and claimed the land for Spain. During the next 200 years, the city would change hands numerous times, and

City of Memphis

ownership would be claimed by the French and the English as well. In 1796, Tennessee became the 16th state admitted to the Union, but the city didn't officially come into existence until more than 20 years later. In 1818, the Chickasaw Indians sold the land to the United States government, and three Tennesseans decided to incorporate a new town.

Future United States President Andrew Jackson and two other entrepreneurs – John Overton and James Winchester – saw the financial possibilities of having a city on the bluffs. The men decided to call the place Memphis, which translates roughly into "place of good abode." The city was officially incorporated in 1826, and played host mainly to river workers and folks who were on their way to the West. In the 1840s, the city began to boom, thanks mainly to the "white gold," or "King Cotton" that was growing in nearby farmlands. By 1850, Memphis was the largest inland cotton market in the world, an industry that relied on the inhumane foundation of slavery. The city's location and its reliance on slave labor would prove to be a volatile mix in the near future.

City of Memphis

Memphians were firmly entrenched on the side of the Confederacy during the Civil War. In 1861, recruits from the city formed more than 70 Confederate companies. Only a year later, the Battle of Memphis took place – a 90-minute fight between the Confederate gunboats and the Union Naval forces – and the Confederate flag flying over the city was taken down and replaced with a United States flag. The Union Army's victory and subsequent occupation as a hospital post for more than 5,000 Union soldiers was beneficial to the city after the war ended, as the Union forces had no need to torch

City of Memphis

the city or terrorize its citizens since the battle was over so quickly. Memphis rebounded quickly from the war, as many merchants realized that the "Yankee" money was actually worth more to them than Confederate money.

Memphis' prime location along the Mississippi River was one of the reasons for its early success, but it also contributed to the city's first failure. The city didn't enjoy the sanitary conditions that it does today and much of the area was prone to flooding, which led to the breeding of mosquitoes. During the yellow fever epidemic of 1873, 5,000 cases of "yellow jack" were reported, and more than 2,000 deaths. At the start of the summer, the city's population was 40,000 citizens, and 25,000 left before the quarantine two months earlier. Five years later, the epidemic returned stronger than ever and nearly wiped out the entire city. More than 17,600 cases were reported, and 5,100 people perished from the disease. Those who were able fled the city, leaving behind a catastrophic economic situation that forced the city into bankruptcy. Memphis surrendered its charter and was reduced to a state-taxing district in

City of Memphis

1879. Meanwhile, a wealthy black businessman named Robert Church, Sr., began buying up land around town, primarily on Beale Street. He built Church Park and Auditorium as a place specifically for blacks and helped make Beale Street an integral part of daily life for the city's African Americans. His son, Robert Church, Jr., began the NAACP here in 1917, and Solvent Savings Bank, which became the largest black-owned bank in the world by 1921. The park named in his honor is still on Beale Street.

As the 19th century ended, Memphis' remaining leaders made plans to restore the city to its glory days, beginning with a new sewer system and tapping the artesian wells deep beneath the city for pure, clean drinking water. Additional infrastructure improvements were made as well, so the city was greeting the 20th century with optimism and hope.

E.H. Crump ruled Memphis as mayor for only six years (1909-1915), but his legacy was felt for many years to come. Crump promised to clean up the city and set about clamping down on

City of Memphis

saloons, gambling and prostitution. Actually, Crump merely used this as a campaign tactic, and vice continued to thrive throughout the city. William Christopher "W.C." Handy was hired to write a campaign song for E.H. "Boss" Crump, and in 1912 he changed the wording of the piece and published "Memphis Blues," the first blues song ever published in America. Handy, considered to be the Father of the Blues, also went on to publish the "St. Louis Blues" and "Beale Street Blues;" the three were tremendously popular blues songs throughout the century.

It was Beale Street where the locals went to find anything and everything legal and illegal. In addition to dice games, houses of ill repute and other wicked diversions, Beale was home to a number of music clubs. Workers who toiled in the hot dusty cotton fields all week would come to Beale Street on the weekend in search of good times and good music. They didn't have to look far. They brought with them the chanting songs, called "field hollers." W.C. Handy was the first to put pen to paper and record these songs and their "blue" notes, and an enduring American art form was born.

City of Memphis

In 1916, the modern supermarket was born in Memphis as local entrepreneur Clarence Saunders opened Piggly Wiggly, the first self-serve grocery store. Within seven years, there were more than 2,600 Piggly Wiggly stores across the country and Saunders had become a millionaire. During the early '20s, he began building himself a 22-room, pink marble mansion – dubbed the Pink Palace – which he eventually lost, along with his company and all of his millions. Today the mansion belongs to the city of Memphis and has been turned into a museum, planetarium and CTI 3D Giant Theater.

City of Memphis

Like other cities across the nation, Memphis was hit hard by the Depression. The country's entry into World War II provided the city with a much-needed influx of commerce and industry thanks to a strong cotton market and the city's numerous defense-related industries. Memphis provided WWII with one of its most enduring symbols – the Memphis Belle, the first B-17 bomber to successfully complete 25 missions over Europe. The plane and its crew logged more than 20,000 combat miles, all without a single casualty. The bomber was named for Margaret Polk, a Memphis sweetheart of the plane's pilot, Robert Morgan.

Throughout the 1940s, Beale Street was home to black musicians who brought the cotton field hollers into the juke joints and clubs. A few blocks off Beale, WDIA became the first radio station in the country that had an all-black format and black disc jockeys. Rufus "Funky Chicken" Thomas and legendary blues man Riley "B.B." King were DJs on the historic station, and both began recording at Sun Studio in the 1950s.

During the early 1950s, a young white boy from the nearby Lauderdale Courts housing project was always hanging around the clubs, and succeeded in soaking up the very styles and essence of Beale Street. The young man named Elvis Presley would stand in the doorways of the clubs begging the owners to let him in, then spend all night listening to them play and copying their styles. He even copied the way the flashy musicians dressed and bought his clothes at the same Beale Street men's store, Lansky Brothers. Later, Elvis took what he learned from the Beale Street musicians and used it when he recorded

City of Memphis

"That's All Right Mama" at Sam Phillips' Sun Studio located a few miles east of Beale Street. Sun Studio recorded a number of then-unknown musicians in the 1950s, including Roy Orbison, Carl Perkins, Johnny Cash, Jerry Lee Lewis, Howling' Wolf and Ike Turner. In fact, Turner's band, which included Jackie Brenston as vocalist, is credited with recording the first rock 'n' roll record at Sun Studio, "Rocket 88."

By the mid-1960s, Memphis had begun the slow process of integrating many of the city's public facilities, but tensions

City of Memphis

exploded during the city's sanitation workers' strike in 1968. Striking sanitation workers wore signs that read "I AM A MAN," and Dr. Martin Luther King, Jr. came to the city to lend his support to the workers' cause. On the evening of April 3, Dr. King gave his famous "I've Been to The Mountaintop" speech at the Mason Temple and then returned to his hotel. The next day, Dr. King was assassinated while standing outside of his hotel room on the balcony of the Lorraine Motel. In 1991, the Lorraine Motel opened to visitors as the National Civil Rights Museum, which provides a three-dimensional overview of the

City of Memphis

movement. Also that year, Memphis elected its first African-American mayor, Dr. Willie W. Herenton.

During the '50s and '60s, blacks and whites worked together to create some of the most important music in American history. The "Memphis Sound" emerged in 1960 when siblings Jim Stewart and Estelle Axton formed Stax Records. Stax would give voice to such legendary musical artists as Sam & Dave, Isaac Hayes and Otis Redding, and the world would groove to soul classics like "Soul Man," "Hold On, I'm Comin'" and "Sittin' On The Dock of the Bay."

City of Memphis

Another local record label that played a major role in the development of the "Memphis Sound" was Hi Records. HI's artist roster included such notable musicians as Al Green, Ann Peebles and Willie Mitchell, and provided the world with records like "Love & Happiness," "Let's Stay Together" and many others.

Innovation continued throughout the '70s as a young entrepreneur named Frederick W. Smith was working hard to create a transportation service that would take advantage of Memphis' centralized location to speed up the transportation of goods. The result of his efforts, FedEx, has changed the way the world does business and contributes more than 32,000 jobs to the local economy.

In 1977 Elvis Presley, the King of Rock 'n' Roll, died at Graceland, his home in the Whitehaven neighborhood. Thousands of mourners turned out to pay their respects to Elvis, lining the street of what is now known as Elvis Presley Boulevard. During the next five years, thousands of fans would make the pilgrimage to Graceland just to stand outside and be near their idol. In 1982 the executor of Elvis' estate, his ex-wife Priscilla Presley, opened the home and grounds to visitors who could tour the king's mansion and pay their respects at his burial site, called the Meditation Garden. Graceland now stands as one of the most popular tourist destinations in the world, welcoming more than 600,000 visitors each year. That number peaks during the summer months, when daily attendances reach more than 4,000.

In the early 1990s, Beale Street made a comeback as a tourist destination and entertainment

City of Memphis

district with clubs offering live music seven days a week. The entertainment district continued to flourish throughout the decade and was voted the second most popular entertainment district in the country. Every year, Beale Street and Downtown's Tom Lee Park are transformed into a sea of music, pork and people during the Memphis in May International Festival. This month-long celebration draws tens of thousands of visitors every spring and features the world-famous Beale Street Music Festival, World Championship Barbecue Cooking Contest and several international

City of Memphis

events honoring a different foreign country every year.

In 2000, Memphis made major league strides in the world of professional sports as the city opened AutoZone Park, a brand-new retro-style ballpark for the AAA affiliate of the St. Louis Cardinals baseball team, the Memphis Redbird

Also in 2000, Memphis welcomed a new NBA team to town, as the Vancouver basketball franchise relocated to the city and became the Memphis Grizzlies. Originally housed in The Pyramid, the team eventually moved to Beale Street

City of Memphis

and FedEx Forum. The $250-million arena opened in September 2004 and hosts not only the Grizzlies, but also the University of Memphis Tigers men's basketball team.

Since the celebration of the 50th Anniversary of Rock 'n' Roll (July 5, 2004 -- the same date that Elvis recorded his first record, "That's All Right," at the legendary Sun Studio), it has become increasingly clear that one of Memphis' greatest attractions to tourists is its incredible music history. Area attractions include Sun Studio, Graceland, the Smithsonian's Rock 'n' Soul Museum, Gibson Guitar

Factory, the Center for Southern Folklore, the Historic Beale Street Entertainment District and Stax Museum of American Soul Music.

After Stax Records went bankrupt in 1976, the studio was sold to a local church and demolished in 1989. In 1998 a group of concerned citizens and philanthropists lead a nonprofit effort to

purchase the property with plans to benefit the Souls Ville neighborhood. Construction began on the museum in 2001, and it opened its doors in May 2003. The 17,000-square-foot museum now

City of Memphis

houses more than 2,000 cultural artifacts celebrating the music made famous by Otis Redding; Booker T. and the MGs; Isaac Hayes; the Bar-Kays; Al Green; Aretha Franklin; Earth, Wind & Fire; and other artists, and was the epicenter for the 50th Anniversary of Soul Music in 2007.

Today Memphis is home to a revitalized downtown area, which includes a variety of tourist destinations; new residential and commercial development; and the restoration of many historic buildings. It continues its focus of

City of Memphis

improving downtown with plans to revitalize the historic riverfront area, Beale Street Landing

Reflecting back on the days when our grandfather would arise every morning around 4:00 am and travel from Covington, Tennessee to The Shelby County Penal Farm for over 30 years; places my mind back to the "good old days". The economy was much prosperous and plentiful. People enjoyed making a living when resources were plentiful. Memphis always had an attraction for crime. But the crime rate was kept at a minimal. There were major corporations which were truly successful and flourishing. Business was at the peak of its height in the days of the 80's. But then all of a sudden!

City of Memphis

Leadership

Counts

City of Memphis

A great leader makes a good impact on the people. A leader must lead the people from where he or she is and not from where they came.

If we choose to vote in a leader whom has experienced poverty issues and not overcame is or her issues mentally; more than likely he or she will manage their government as how they were reared and brought up. A strong mental capacity is essential for great authority.

How can a leader lead anyone to a well and he or she hasn't had anything to drink him or herself?

It's okay to remanence on some challenges which we've had to incur in the past. But it's not so good if the mindset hasn't elevated or changed from those circumstances.

I haven't voted in the past and not a Shelby county resident. But I am aware that a fresh watered mind can bring fresh watered results. So let's say for instance that I Tom grew up in a home where he had to share a bedroom with siblings and didn't have many luxuries which his parents would've loved to have had. Tom makes a difference and change over the years by attending college and becomes a successful engineer. Tom has received the big break of his life as he didn't have when he was a child. Tom goes on to begin and family with a successful lawyer and they are now living at the peak of their lifestyle. Tom goes in to work one day and receives some bad news. His finds out that his department is downsizing and that his role as a lead engineer gets cut. Instead of Tom picking up the scraps and not being knowledgeable of what he already has; his mindset goes back to the poverty stage of failure from whence he came. He never took the opportunity to plan for any setbacks in life. He forgot about his wife was a prominent attorney in the entire state. He wasn't versed of how to move forward. And this is why leadership is so very important. It's okay to not have had the finest things in life growing up. But any leader should have a mindset to be a thinker and not a failure. I can recall our grandfather driving over 75 miles daily round-trip to Memphis. He didn't allow the fact that there weren't any jobs in Covington, Tennessee to detour him from providing for the household. He got up and made it

City of Memphis

happen. And this is where leadership has fallen in the great city. Men aren't aware of how to relocate or travel the extra mile in order to have a stable living. But instead they shift the blame at those whom are in political office for their failures. The failures start in the mindset. No one is responsible for another man's success. He or she is responsible for their own accomplishments and achievements. Women are the most prone to ask for something. But now we see that the hands of men are held out more than the women in this great city. Men were led to lead and not to beg. God has fashioned man in a way that man can ask for things and they are provided instantaneously. Why? Because men were commissioned by God to provide (Genesis 2 & 3).

So Tom begins to decline in his self-pity and is embarrassed to speak to his wife about his declining employment. If you noticed in the scenario that Tom's job was downsizing and his position would be cut. The scenario *never* said that Tom would lose his job. Do you see where I'm going with this. Many times we aren't reflecting on the fact that we still have something. And we must work hard for a higher achievement. Sometimes a set-back is a blessing in disguise. All bad news is not bad. It can work for your good if you know how to utilize your time and mindset. If our mindset can become distracted from where we can and not where we are; this will allow failure to play a major role in our thinking. Leadership begins in the home. If you're not a good leader in the home; then how can you run a political office or function properly in the workforce industry. This is why it is so important to know whom you are voting for. Do your homework on candidates whom are running for office? If you don't have a computer; purchase a newspaper, search your local library catalogues. This will be a huge impact on your future. They were electing this one particular mayor in for the city of Memphis as an interim mayor. This occurred when they had the "weird guy" Mango running for mayor. I recalled a question which was elected for interim stating that "He would take a paid company car which was provided by the City of Memphis knowing that the city was already in financial trouble. I'm not quoting the question correctly. But the term is correct. It has been a few years back. Once this particular mayor; whom I don't want to name stated Yes; he would

City of Memphis

accept a paid company car from the expenses of the city of Memphis; knowing that the city was already in financial decline; I knew that the city was in trouble then. This told me that this mayor was seeking personal gain for himself and wasn't interested in the people's concerns. This is what I mean by having a poverty state of mind. This particular mayor grew up African American and he was somewhat poor. But he built himself to where he could build a better lifestyle and career for himself and his family. This is good; but you cannot run a city or conglomerate based from your past. This is how some city governments decline financially. They pace or vote the wrong candidate into office whom may have degrees and a successful career. But the mindset is very important of whom you are electing in. African Americans in the city of Memphis vote according to race and not discernment. Life wasn't created for all African Americans or any race to have a free living and free handouts. There were challenges and obstacles in which many great men from The Bible had to face daily and we weren't created to live for free. Our lifestyle living originated from a middle class home and this was due to our grandfather and grandmother making strategic decisions. Our grandfather only made it to the 2nd grade and our grandmother to the 8th; but they had more credit cards and charge account that I would desire to own. This is because of their mindset. We never heard our grandfather complain once about driving all those miles to and from Memphis. We never heard our grandmother complaining about her responsibilities of ironing, and dusting in homes of others. They worked and was satisfied at what they had. We had a good up brining and never experienced food and necessity shortages in the home. They always made sure that they were good providers for the family. This is how men and women can become great leaders and not "baby-bibbers." I feel strongly that leaders need to work in their own field of work and remain there. If I'm a business owner and I have the inclination to run for a political office; I really need to make sure am I the right fit for the city. A great leaders know how to handle obstacles of they arise. He or she may not know everything; but I feel that god will give them knowledge of how to handle the issue. I served on a library board once in another county. The citizens were requesting amenities for the children in the area such as more computers and so on. Well the mayor of that town didn't see a need for all that nor did he see a need for change. Why? Because all of his children were grown. So if you elect an official which doesn't see the views and opinions of other; then change will be irrelevant for that area. This is why he was de-thronged and another mayor was elected. Because people get tired of "junky leadership." Junky Leadership is someone whom has a name and title and wears it perfuse; but doesn't have the knowledge of how to manage government; see others opinions and views, etc.

This is why the teen issue has grown in the city of Memphis. If leadership doesn't have small kids or haven't had troubled issues within their own lifetime; they will not know how to manage anyone else's. I never saw on the news of how a strategy was set in place for the outrage violence of teens in this city. The new elected mayor has embarked upon some hard challenges which was left upon him by poor leaderships prior to him being elected into office. This is why race shouldn't be a factor for voting or electing someone into office. The individual can and will have their own personal affects as a priority and not the people.

City of Memphis

Bringing jobs into the city of Memphis doesn't make any official a good leader. Where is the training? Where is the Education? Where is the knowledge? We must learn something first. I'm not referring to the knowledge of taking up course in college to get free grant money that you will soon have to pay back. There is nothing for free! Because I can have a college degree but this doesn't qualify me for the job. Employers are seeking out good communication skills, they' re wandering if they hire he or she how will this build asset for their company. People aren't just hiring because of degrees. Again; the mindset of how we think. The last twenty years' people have been excited about the great city of Memphis because they felt that someone was going to give them a free ticket to *Heaven.* But only to find out that the City of Memphis had declined in recent years in many areas of economics and social living. This is how Olive Brach and other cities built their luxurious estates. Once a poverty state of mind in leadership enters; then those of a seasoned mind will move away. They have a right to. Why? Because this decreases property value for home owners and crime will also run seasoned mind setters away. Leadership and how it is governed can change an entire government.

Prayer

City of Memphis

Prayer is a must for any success on Earth. We don't have to be noticed or acknowledged as a prayer warrior. All we need to do is to place this into practice and allow prayer to remain there. This doesn't mean that we should pray on the streets or pray openly on our jobs, nor pray openly in the schools. God will answer and hear our prayers in the quietness places. These are some excuses which individuals have made because of the declining of Memphis. God looks on the heart of man and not the outer appearance. Make prayer a daily essential for home, career, church, business, etc. And you will see things change. Schools aren't responsible for praying for your change. Although; it's a huge plus for anything in our social and economic living. But Deuteronomy 11 states its best. "And ye shall teach them your children, speaking of them when thou sittest in thine house, and when thou walkest by the way, when thou liest down, and when thou risest up.

20 And thou shalt write them upon the door posts of thine house, and upon thy gates:

21 That your days may be multiplied, and the days of your children, in the land which the LORD sware unto your fathers to give them, as the days of heaven upon the earth.

22 For if ye shall diligently keep all these commandments which I command you, to do them, to love the LORD your God, to walk in all his ways, and to cleave unto him. So as we can view by these scriptures; that the responsibility is with the parent for learning Christianity and prayer. The parent; according to God's laws are the ones whom should be the first

teach in the morning and before the child lies down to go to bed. This is when you know that an area is experiencing issues; when others begin the blame-game.

Parents perhaps haven't been taught themselves which can cause a ripple effect in the home and generation. They aren't aware of how to pray themselves and desire others to do the hard work that is their own responsibility. This also causes the dependency factor to creep in. Some parents haven't experienced a father or mother figure themselves. So they aren't aware to turn to for help or know how to put on their "big man or woman pants" to manage and operate a household. Prayer begins in the home. If laws and rules change in society; this doesn't have any reflection on how successful, your child is in the school systems. This is just another crutch for poverty-thinkers to have pity on themselves. Again; just another excuse.

Education

City of Memphis

Education is one of the easiest things which we can have for success. Everyone isn't college pronged. But you can begin a legacy or build a career from the ground up. I recall working as a sandwich maker in my earlier years. I was always dedicated to my work and always on time. This is something which my grandfather embedded in us. We lived about 3 minutes from the church down the highway. Sunday school would begin at 9:30 am and we would always leave the house at 9:00 am going to church. It was right down the highway. But our grandfather never wanted to be late for church or work. He car-pooled with

City of Memphis

another deacon from our church to *The Shelby County Penal Farm.* The deacon had more children which brought more responsibility for the car-pooler. So sometimes he would over sleep. Our house phone was directly beside my bed. And I could recall my grandfather having to call him at times to remind him that they were going to be late. The wife would always answer the phone and speak for the car-pooler. But our grandfather would tell her to tell him that he was gone. He couldn't be late because the car-pooler over-slept. Good leaders always rise up early in the morning. No man doesn't have any business getting out of bed no later than 7:00 am. He should be the thinker, the resolver, the mastermind of the home and for business. A leader should always keep him or herself acclimated with news, statistics, and reports of daily issues or daily activities which surrounds him or her.

If one doesn't possess the financial funding at the time to attend college; he or she can remain in "The Know" by healthy relationships and environment. As the old saying goes *"You are what you eat."* The same goes for your colleagues and friends. You are and become whom your environment is evolved around.

Have you ever known a person having one particular voice and later on in years their accent or tone has changed? The reason for this is their environment. Healthy Relationships are good for success and opportunities. Reflecting back on a particular individual whom attended college for journalism. She excelled in her courses. She met an individual whom was college versed as well. But he had an issue with substance abuse of drinking which compelled her to this abuse. They were united in matrimony, but the relationship declined later on in years. She had to convert back to her parents. Now this is fine if you need to go

City of Memphis

back and regroup, but you have to use the mindset of your noggin to continue persevering. She didn't do this. She moved back without a plan. Her parents passed away and now she was left alone. She began to surround herself around those whom didn't originate from her background status and this caused her lifestyle and potential to decline. While attending college or any type of training; make sure that you have a plan and keep a healthy environment so that you will continue to excel. Good relationships can catapult you in the right direction for progression. ***Back to the Sandwich-Maker***: So with the former job which I had; I was a sandwich maker. My attendance and character moved me up to team leader. Later on I became Assistant Manager and considered for General Manager opportunities. Many times a career will not begin with a certificate or degree. It will begin with character building. There were managers whom were exiting the college world and hired in the same field which I was employed at a restaurant in the City of Memphis and my pay was much higher than the other college employer. Good characterization can open good doors for you. I learned more with the job in the restaurant industry by taking training sessions and seminars.

I wanted to grow with the company and learn more before I changed occupations. You see I've worked in this great city back in the 90's and left in the year 2000. I've worked in every location of the city and there was and still is great opportunities. Opportunities are based upon ones' education level and knowledge. This is what the church leaders and school systems should be sharing with the teens as they prepare for them for success. There are jobs in the City of Memphis? But do the applicant or citizen have the education to become an employee for the job? Once again; this goes back to the mindset.

There is no employer which is going to hire someone on a prominent job without healthy credentials. How can one provide asset and stability for a company if they don't read, study, become acclimated with things around their society, build, save, set? The jobs are there. But the education prohibits one for accessing the prize. As I type this book; I've never had any typing skills. I learned by utilizing a computer and from prior employments which required computer skills. My ability to type grew more and more. I sought out positions within my employers which required clerical skills to build more skills. Education is a must if you desire to succeed. You have to pick up a newspaper, watch the news, educational programs on television, wall street journals, read a financial report, etc. The ball is in the court of the potential one and not anyone else. Change would need to be in effect in order to expect change. It begins with the mind.

Employment

City of Memphis

Excuses aren't a reason for not having a job. The responsibility isn't on the economy either; it goes back to your education and how much you are willing to invest with your future. Many times an individual desire to make a larger paying rate without the skills or education. Certain crimes and felonies will detour some applicants from possessing certain careers. But I've learned from past reviews; that there are many agencies and non-profits in the City of Memphis which can assets those whom have criminal records to find a job. Some applicants or picky choosers. Employment is available; but they desire to pick-and-choose what they like. And this is okay. But you have to "crawl-before-you-walk." You may have to take some things in order to receive greater things. But back to the mindset; some don't see the equation of this great formula. I've seen and experienced as a manager in Memphis; employees bringing their friends and family onto the property areas of the business while they were on the time clock. This can also result to a negative feedback in hiring for employment. Employers are weary of hiring those whom create chaos in the workforce or a busy lifestyle on their company property. Employees are hired to work and

City of Memphis

not to hang-out on the premises with friends and family. It's not the city officials' responsibility to provide a job for anyone. You can begin a fresh start by formulating a great plan for success, cleaning up the environment in which her or she resides, connect with a local clergy, and begin the process for a successful future. If gang activity was an issue in the past; there is always a way out. City leaders shouldn't encourage those whom aren't succeeding in their future to blame others for their present status. Leaders should encourage them and gear then in the right direction. We didn't come through life with a "golden spoon" in our mouths. Our grandfather possessed the means, but we went to assist elderly people in their homes as well. We were paid for dusting, cleaning *China – Ware,* raking leaves, and more. This provided a path of independency for ourselves. We learned the value of a dollar at the age of 12, not 25.

It's an epitome to see and hear grown men whimper and complain as babies.

Marketing for Business

City of Memphis

Marketing and training is a must for business owners. With our non-profit organization; we have seen less impact om businesses or programs teaching entrepreneurs how to become independent successors. With the last six years; I have attended workshops, conferences, and events which reflect on women achieving through contract bids, 501 3 filings and for profit business. These says to me that a minority business can withhold its own unless it has one of these credentials as a licensee. And we have held workshops in the City of Memphis to attempt to turn this statistic around. There is no assistance support or help for those of nonprofits; only for profits. S.C.O.R.E of Memphis; which I am member of; has an exception platform of providing mentoring and help to those whom may need to learn how to create a business plan. This was the purpose of joining the team. I wanted to help those whom may need assistance in areas of building a branding their business. A small idea results into a large idea. As the scripture states; "Despise not small beginning" Zechariah 4:10. We also create monthly magazines to empower and impact our business. A beginning author submitted some images for the magazine. I first thought to reject the offer due to his attire. But I quickly remembered how it was to struggle with building a business from the ground and approved the opportunity. He was an African American man whom was changing his career by authoring books. I felt that this would be the only door which he felt that couple open for him. So I allowed him to share his new book release in our magazine as a paid advertiser. Programs and seminars should be set in place for those whom re non profiteers for success. There will be times when the entrepreneur will need to search out information as well; but having some type of platform can allow them to grow and the city will grow for success. I had an opportunity to interview The CEO of Garment-Exchange. Her company is an online clothes rental. I would've never thought about this. But as we know in the path of millennium thinkers; small businesses are growing rapidly. You have to provide some resources for the citizens to activate their potential. It's not giving the resources to them for free because they are transporting to and from the area to retrieve the knowledge. There is nothing free. Things have become so critical that officials are making decisions on charging a fee for those whom enter the city. I'm aware of toll fees and how beneficial this can be for the city. But the City of Memphis will gain more for allowing traders, merchants, and potential customers to purchase more than those tool fees. It starts with a mind strategy. Go back and search out how did you get to where you are now. If we learn how to dig and clean out the root of a situation; this will prevent the situation from occurring. Get rid of the problem so that there is continue flow and access for others. I think that Memphis was actually tired of the same old results from previous leaders and decided to elect a new face. I prayed that Mayor Jim

Strickland would win the election. Although I've never been a citizen of Memphis; but have been employed and still build business owners by hosting monthly workshops in the area. Jim Strickland will be the man whom makes change in this area and bring more success and potential for the citizens.